T0197194

Raw

KAREN LEE STRADFORD

BALBOA.PRESS
A DIVISION OF HAY HOUSE

Balboa Press books may be ordered through booksellers or by contacting:

Balboa Press
A Division of Hay House
1663 Liberty Drive
Bloomington, IN 47403
www.balboapress.com
844-682-1282

Because of the dynamic nature of the Internet, any web addresses or
links contained in this book may have changed since publication and
may no longer be valid. The views expressed in this work are solely those
of the author and do not necessarily reflect the views of the publisher,
and the publisher hereby disclaims any responsibility for them.

The author of this book does not dispense medical advice or prescribe the use
of any technique as a form of treatment for physical, emotional, or medical
problems without the advice of a physician, either directly or indirectly. The
intent of the author is only to offer information of a general nature to help
you in your quest for emotional and spiritual well-being. In the event you use
any of the information in this book for yourself, which is your constitutional
right, the author and the publisher assume no responsibility for your actions.

Any people depicted in stock imagery provided by Getty Images are
models, and such images are being used for illustrative purposes only.
Certain stock imagery © Getty Images.

Print information available on the last page.

ISBN: 979-8-7652-3596-6 (sc)
ISBN: 979-8-7652-3597-3 (e)

Library of Congress Control Number: 2022920074

Balboa Press rev. date: 10/31/2022

Synopsis

My book Raw is about self-reflection and embracing the inner-self. I tell a story about my life through each poem- sharing my personal experiences when dealing with grief, love, happiness and sadness. I immediately found great comfort and healing by writing poems after the sudden death of my father on October 10, 2021. I hope that my poems will inspire others to look within themselves and share their own stories.

Acknowledgement

I would like to thank my loving parents Eliza A. and Lillian M., as well as my sister Dr. Lynn M. Stradford for always encouraging me to express myself through writing poems.

Contents

Raw

Liberate yourself.
Speak your mind.
Start each day
with a new outlook,
but never forget
your past.

Bitterness will try to
hold on
and
leave a nasty stain.
Celebrate a resilient you,
instead.

Daddy

The light shines on your face
as you lie in the cobalt casket
your spirit simmers,
eternal.

Our pleasant conversations
over Chock Full O' Nuts, bagels and scrambled eggs
as Channel 2 news rouses the activities of the day.

My fierce advocate, like a builder
repairing a difficult task,
your strength gives me comfort and guidance.

As the sun continues to rise,
your heavenly presence will forever stir throughout-
my life.

Vine

You grow on me like a
fresh vine strangling a weathered tree
your grip so tight
I cannot move.

So, I flounder.

You loosen your grip
just enough to let me breathe
I exhale
and realize.

Tar Wheels

It is a hot summer day.
I pull out of my freshly paved driveway
riding along listening to music,
my elbow poking out of the window.
Not a care in the world, I change lanes to weave between
the traffic.

Suddenly, the sky opens up to a drizzle then a heavy
downpour. I am pissed that my perfect scenery is fading.
I rush to roll up.

The cars nearby start to brake.
I quickly try to slow down,
but I can feel my car bounce before the pedal lowers
completely to the floor.
Without warning, I am trapped while my car propels me
into a continuous spin.

I panic,
and look for a way out.
Around and round I go
what feels like an endless cycle.
I'm thinking that help is sure to come.

The rain stops
and the car is no longer spinning
on the highway.
Nervously, I exit my car to discover
dried tar.

Crisis

The world
in a terrible state,
peace, love and happiness is-
lost.

Like a bumpy, gravel road,
life is difficult to maneuver,
negative vibes are ahead.

At war with ourselves,
weapons are everywhere
as hate speech surrounds.

The pain is killing us,
people don't seem to panic.

Civility, please
show your friendly face
before it's too late.

On My Mind

I wake up with a lot
on my mind,
thinking about things
from
the day before.

I'm not ready to
leave my bed and
face the crowd.
I reach for the
writing tablet
on the nightstand
for a companion.

Like being on a date
with my thoughts,
I reflect
and
hope
someone else
will understand.

Homeless

Open your heart.
Show kindness and let someone in-
that person who has nothing to eat
and nowhere to sleep.
Shelter is their necessity.

It's hard to imagine a world where
people struggle to survive
in a prosperous land.
Things must get better.

"One hand washes another" my grandpa used to say.

A warm bed, shower,
clean clothes and a hot meal
can restore a person's dignity.

Live Music Feeds The Soul

It's been a long day.
I can use a distraction.
My sister Lynn invited me to an
outdoor concert,
guaranteed to make me forget my troubles
and lose myself in the music.

With no questions asked, I prepare for the greatest show
on earth.
I imagine the smell of fresh cut grass, covered with
colorful blankets
and folding chairs, drenched by the sun.

People from all over the park gather around me,
as the band plays my favorite song.
In that moment, I dance to the steady beat of the drums
and the piercing strum of the electric guitars.

My body is transforming,
elevating at least 10 feet off the ground
as I feel the force of the sounds take me to another
dimension.

No troubles in sight.
For that short moment in time,
my soul is well fed.

Rejection

The years we spend together
break us further apart.

We always travel a careful, smooth road,
but never share the same destination.

Over time, our feelings seem to yield
after happiness
and heartbreak.

I realize I
will be better
on my own.

Glitch

I'm excited about voting,
as I drive to the polls.
Despite the drizzle,
I didn't mind standing in line
for the guard to let us in.

Already confident of my choice,
a man hands me red and blue
flyers, postcards.
I accept with a smile.

A lady waves me to her computer,
searches for my name.
I wait,
and wait,
and wait.
Growing anxious,
wondering about
my status.

She's puzzled,
not sure what to say.
Screen swivels.
I brace myself.
1870.

Secret Death

We grew up together,
next door neighbors.
Our siblings close in ages, like steps.

We were always full of life,
playing hide and seek in the backyard,
running around the bases
and riding our bikes
to the corner store for snacks.

We flourished in school-
meeting new friends
and working.
Then, alcoholism took
its toll on you.

I still see your brother and sister daily,
greeting them with a wave,
smile and
small talk.
I ask how you're doing,
seeking a full status report.

Now, I'm very emotional,
as I reminisce
about our childhood.

No one told me.
You died
last week.

Reminisce

Today is a very uneventful one.
I'm home alone looking for a way to pass the time.
Walking around my bedroom,
I spot a Tupperware container
filled with random things.

I lift the lid,
scoop to the bottom
and found pictures of myself wearing
ballet and jazz costumes.
I wish they could still fit.

Photos of my grandparents are black and white
with hints of coffee stains.
I turn them over to find the year.
Their expressions appear solemn,
like they had the weight of the world
on their shoulders.

I dig deeper
and pull out a glossy 8x10.
I remember shopping for the perfect black and gold gown
with 4 inch heels.
Suddenly, I feel like a princess again.

I haven't seen my prince
in 20 years,
wonder how he's doing since we
lost touch.

My cell phone rings.
I answer
and hear
a familiar voice.

Dirt Bike

I'm 16 today.
I got a dirt bike.
After years of asking, I knew that my parents would
finally give in.
I can't wait to
cruise.
The envy of my friends.

First thing I need is to learn to drive.
At the park, my dad showed me the features.
Eagerly, I ride
through the paths,
around the pond,
up and down the small hills.

My confidence is fading,
can't remember how to
stop.
I gain rapid speed
heading towards the bottom,
picnic table in sight.

My dad,
a superhero.

The Blue Shed

It's midday.
The town is active.
I sit at the long,
red light
watching intently
as people
wearing fancy face masks
walk on Springfield Avenue
dodging in
and out
of restaurants
and traffic.

A small blue shed
sits near the sidewalk,
welcoming those
who
might need
to enter.

A young boy
opens the door,
quickly fills
his knapsack
with cans
then leaves
with
a smile.

The Fight

I said his name
during our
shouting match.
I'm sorry.
I know I hurt you.

I had no idea
my feelings for him
are so
strong.

But, you
will not listen
unless I raise
my voice.

The Storm

The air is changing, the sun shifts,
the wind gains speed, and twirls around me
as I frantically run towards the house.

Hurry to close the windows
and pull the Levolor blinds,
desperate to secure my place in the bedroom.

The sky begins to snap, crackle, pop and the lightning
strikes the window
faster and faster as I dive, cowardly under my firm bed
and lay horizontal to the wall.
The thunder pounds faster and faster as
I cover my ears
wondering when this sudden disturbance in my daily
routine will stop.
I can't wait to see the sun again.

The forces appear to weaken as
I remain stuck to the floor.

Proof of calm is needed
before I can move.

Therapy

I'm scared,
not sure what to expect
when I walk into the room.
I slowly glance around,
paranoid, as a sea of eyes
stare back at me.

Never thought
I would need therapy,
hoping the pain would go away.

Feeling vulnerable
like a damsel in distress,
I sit alone on the
soft bench with my tears
at a loss for words.

Mike approaches
with a dixie cup of water
and a calm voice.
Assured me.
I will be fine.

Thick Skin

Words can hurt.
At times cut
like a sharp knife,
more powerful than
physical force.

Verbal harm
can penetrate the mind,
an attempt to lower self-esteem
and question your worthiness.

Like an unplugged microphone,
I tune out what you're saying.
Meanness has no platform here.

Each lesson
teaches me how to
navigate through life
and ignore negativity.
My skin is thick.

Loving Mom

Lillian Maria-
You're the first person
to show me
true love,
teach me
to respect myself,
others
and worship God.

My best friend-
It's difficult to express exactly
how much you mean to me.
Somehow, no adjective seems suitable.
You're a proud lady who knows
she's blessed
and leads by example.

Like a gentle force of nature,
your dignity and strong presence
can fill any room.
Your comfort and helpful advice
is one of a kind.

I celebrate you with flowers
while you can smell them,
add to your garden
of love.

Game

I try to fit into your life
like a forgotten puzzle piece,
to find a place of belonging
and hopes of sharing things.
Every day,
my position, difficult.
It feels like a task.
Never a part of the plan
to include me

in your circle.

Rescue

Somehow, you knew I needed you.
You found me when I was lost.

My weakness was so obvious.
You refused to leave my side.

I depended on you to come around.
After all, cats are curious.
I know that I found a true friend.
A new home is what you found.

Second Chance

It's a day I won't forget.
I saw Darrin
for the first time
in many years.

Life has been hard on him.
Drug abuse and
time spent in prison
had taken its toll.

Trouble seemed
to follow,
everywhere.
He realized
bad choices
were made.

Like a diamond in the rough
with obstacles in the past,
Darrin longs for
another chance to
succeed.

I'm proud of him.

Duck

Let the worries
roll off your back,
like a duck
in water.

Positive thoughts
and meditation
gently ease
the stress of the day.

Wade in a stream
of hope.

Childless

Some things in life are puzzling to me.
I spent many days wondering why I wasn't blessed with a
child
to love and nourish,
call my own,
guide through life
and provide for.

Somehow, it was never the right season
for me to welcome
another person into the world.
But, I believe that God had his reason.

Jimi Hendrix Motivates Me

My alarm clock plays
Purple Haze.
I hit the snooze button
four times.

I sit on the side of my bed
think about what to wear,
look for motivation
to start my day.

I walk across the room
to my closet full of concert t-shirts,
open the door and
slide the hangers
to the right.

As I move them,
in my mind
I can hear Jimi tell me
to choose his.

I wrestle with
the thought of
choosing someone else
because I just wore him
yesterday.

I, finally,
slip Jimi's shirt
off the hanger,
and imagine him
saying-
now, you're ready
to have
a groovy one.

Like Broken Glass

Friday evenings are precious,
especially after a long week at work.
I plan to indulge in my leisure time.

With so many activities on the agenda,
I decide to go shopping
then catch a bite to eat with friends,
belly full of comfort food,
I opt for aluminum to-go containers.

Before leaving,
I tell everyone to stay safe.

Arriving home, I carefully juggle my bundles
not prepared for what's about to happen.

Unaware of the small red rug
on the garage floor,
I trip
and fall.

My evening is
spoiled.

Kneecap shattered,
broken glass.

Look Out for Others

I bounce
out of my car
like a pinky ball
in a hurry
and down the sidewalk
I see a petite figure
in the distance,
walking slowly
towards me.

The image
moves in an
unbalanced rhythm
pushing a small cart.
So, I wait.

An elderly woman is in view,
wearing a blue dress with a
polka-dot headscarf and sandals,
hunched over
her bundles.

She gets closer.
I offer
assistance.

She said,
she'll be fine
just help the people
in Ukraine.

Poetry Over Pizza

It's a good day
to write poetry
in my yard.
The sun is bright,
clear sky,
grass freshly cut.

I invite my friend
to collaborate.
She arrives with a bag
full of papers
and the munchies.

We order pizza
and wait
for our ideas
to flow.

Light up.
The smell
of weed fills the air,
like potpourri.

In a zone,
we share
stanzas,
give

feedback and
relish
in compliments.

The pizza is here.
But now,
we're
too full.

Fast Food

I whip into the parking lot,
anxious to get close to the door.
The large filet meal is
always my choice.
I can't wait to eat
French fries.

Rush in
to join the line,
growing impatient with the
indecisiveness of the woman
before me.
I wonder why she is taking so long.

Finally, it's my turn.
I go to the counter,
eager to place my order.
The friendly cashier asked me what I wanted.
Happy to answer, I tell him what I like.

I step aside
to retrieve my bag.
Somehow, the quick visit seems like
an overnight stay.
I wonder about the hold up.
"Ma'am, 30 minutes."

Heatwave

I'm hot.
I wake up
sweating
after
tossing and turning
in my bed.

I put my feet on the warm,
shaggy red rug.
The air is thick and sticky.
I'm being pushed back
with every step.

I look in the mirror,
my frizzy, wet hair confirms
that the weather report
is accurate.

I panic.
Suddenly, I feel like
I'm trapped
in a furnace.

Turn on the fan.
No relief.

The Waiting Room

It's time for my annual.
I arrive early.
The lot is full.
People look for spots.

I rush through
the revolving door,
run down
the long hall
to catch the elevator
with the light
flashing up.

I jump on eager to press 2.
The floor rocks, like an earthquake.
I grab the bar on the wall.

The waiting room
is crammed.
Chairs face each other.
No one makes
eye contact.
I squeeze
between a pocketbook
and a walker
while balancing
admission forms
on my lap.

The receptionist sits
behind a plastic shield,
reaches under
to retrieve the clipboard.

One hour later-
I wait.

Family Reunion

The annual family reunion
is finally here.
I looked forward to this day.
The date has been penciled
on my calendar for months.
I can't wait
to reconnect.

The sun is beaming.
The air is filled
with the aromas of charcoal,
burgers
and steaks.
Water, beer and soda
are packed in coolers
with crushed ice.

House Music can be heard
throughout the park,
as we dance
to DJ Michael's beats.

I take pictures of everyone
talking,
laughing
and smiling
in various poses.

Now, I'm surrounded by
stacks
of
memories.

Biography

Karen Lee Stradford is currently a certified Special Education/English teacher at Columbia High School in the South Orange and Maplewood School District in New Jersey. She holds a Master's of Arts degree (M.A.) and certifications as a Learning Disabilities Teacher Consultant (LDT/C) and a Supervisor.

Many of her poems are published by: Literary Yard ezine and Scars Publications (Down in the Dirt magazine).

Printed in the United States
by Baker & Taylor Publisher Services